To

From

The God
Who is Still Here

G.P. Haggart

LuLu Press

The God Who is Still Here

Cover art by Greg P. Haggart

Printed in the United States of America

ISBN: 978-1-300-28531-1

The Flammarion engraving depicts a traveler who arrives at the edge of a flat Earth and sticks his head through the firmament.

Imagine

The world use to sit on top of a giant turtle. As the turtle walked or moved there were earthquakes and tidal waves. But the world wasn't always this way. As time went on science further decided that the world was noticeably flat and that going out to far in the ocean would make a ship drop off the world. It wasn't until 1492 when Christopher Columbus against all odds discovered the Americas that science conceded that the world was round.

As hundreds of years went by scholars discovered that an ancient text signaled ahead of time that the world was a sphere shape. Scientists had completely ignored this credit because it came from a religious source. Science took the credit for discovering that the world was a sphere shape even though the Bible spoke about this fact thousands of years ago. Science neglected to look at ancient historical records to find the truth and be enlightened by God. Instead science took the credit away from what God said to Isaiah and claimed the discovery.

Isn't it reasonable for science to look at ancient recorded history to find the truth? To find out what happen or to find out why things are the way they are? Isn't it obvious to look at recorded ancient history as a wise grandfather to find the truth so that we don't jump to conclusions and become foolish? Instead science would have you believe that ancient man was stupid and didn't record anything nor had the ability and resources to listen to a divine being that cared enough to provide knowledge [science]. Instead evolutionary science wants to lead us to believe that humanity forgot our past and that it is their job to find out what happen. The fact is evolutionary science is the reason why humanity is deceived in believing we are an amnesia species. How awesome would it be if mankind would have taken the time to look at the ancient records instead of making up things by his own selfish ego when making discoveries?

So I ask you to put aside your foolish ego for a moment and stop thinking that the world is flat and be like Christopher Columbus and journey further into the pages of this book to find truth. After all you want the truth correct?

Within this book are the most common questions that atheists, agnostics and backsliders ask, and after each of the following statements are answers. You may disagree with it or not but the fact remains that this is the truth. Let us begin and be reasonable.

The Gospel Account Matches Characters of Mythology

This statement refers to the references of mythological characters like Herakles, Asklepios, the Dioscuri, Dionysus, and a dozen others. The claim is that early Christian writers borrowed these stories and attributed them to Jesus Christ when the religion was in formation. This is complete none sense in the form that the early Jewish Christians would take pieces from paganism and apply it to their religion. The Maccabee revolution against the Greeks saw the formation of two very stubborn denominations [the Pharisees and Sadducee] in the aftermath of that rebellion revealed a steadfast doctrinal movement that the Jewish leaders engaged in. Much of the early Christians were Jews who were steadfast in the divine Law of God. The very rule of law surrounding the temple itself pushed pagan visitors into an outer section of the temple. These gentile visitors were not allowed to enter further in the inner sanctuary of the temple.

There are many claims by atheists that the early "mystery religions" had some type of influence upon early Christianity. These mystery religions are a mystery because the inner cult members held secret rituals that weren't known by the early Christians. Much of these rituals involved blood sacrifices for the consecration of priests. We can see that in the taurobolium in the Attis cult is first attested in the time of Antoninus Pius for A.D. 160. The consecration of priests involved.

... The falling shower rains down a foul dew, which the priest buried within catches, putting his shameful head under all the drops, defiled both in his clothing and in all his body.

Yea, he throws back his face, he puts his cheeks in the way of the blood, he puts under it his ears and lips, he interposes his nostrils, he washes his very eyes with the fluid, nor does he even spare his throat but moistens his tongue, until he actually drinks the dark gore.

... The pontiff, horrible in appearance, comes forth, and shows his wet head, his beard heavy with blood, his dripping fillets and sodden garments.

This man, defiled with such contagions and foul with the gore of the recent sacrifice, all hail and worship at a distance, because profane blood and a dead ox have washed him while concealed in a filthy cave.

This passage reveals the consecration of a priest. This type of ritual would repulse any early Jew including a Jewish Christian. One Christian, Prudentius, and his words "foul dew," "shameful head," "defiled both in his clothing and in all his body," indicate that he considered the whole rite to be crude and blasphemous. Since the taurobolium post-dates the New Testament all together, there is no possible way for the early Christians to have adopted this material into Christianity.

The German scholar Gunter Wagner has written the definitive work on Christianity and the mystery religions. In it he explains:

"The taurobolium in the Attis cult is first attested in the time of Antoninus Pius for A.D. 160. As far as we can see at present it only became a personal consecration at the beginning of the third century A.D. The idea of a rebirth through the instrumentality of the taurobolium only emerges in isolated instances toward the end of the fourth century A.D.; it is not originally associated with this blood-bath."

Let's take a look at some ancient heroes that atheists like to use to try and reflect Jesus' life.

Herakles, died by a poisoned shirt laced with Hydra blood by Deianira. She gave it to Herakles' servant Lichas who Herakles thrown into the sea before dying thinking he was the only one who poisoned him. Hereakles was then brought to Mt. Olympus by Zeus where Herakles finally died. Jesus didn't die by a poisoned shirt and when he ascended into heaven he didn't die. Hardly a similar story. Herakles also had a twin brother named Iphicles. Jesus never had a twin brother at the event of his birth. Herakles also begot children, Jesus did not.

Asklepios, the son of Apollo and Coronis. Coronis was killed for being unfaithful. Mary, Jesus' mother wasn't killed and was faithful. Asklepios was killed by Zeus with a thunder bolt for raising Hippolytus from the dead. Jesus was willing to die on the cross and was sentence to die by the Roman authority. When Jesus raised Lazarus from the dead he never accepted any payment, however in the story of Asklepios he accepted payment of gold. Other stories portray Asklepios death very differently. One story says that he died when he raised too many people from the dead and Hades requested Zeus to take his life. The story of Asklepios has variations while the Gospel accounts of Jesus haven't changed.

The Dioscuri, were Castor and Pollux. Yet twins, Castor was the mortal son of Tyndareus, king of Sparta, and Pollux the son of Zeus, who visited the twins' mother Leda in the disguise of a swan. The Gospel of Matthew doesn't tell of a twin brother of Jesus nor does it mention the Holy Spirit as a bird symbol until later in the Gospel accounts of Jesus' baptism. Nor does the New Testament tell that the Holy Spirit "disguises" itself when visiting with the early Christians. The person who visited the Virgin Mary was the Gabriel who informed Mary that she was pregnant with Jesus; Gabriel wasn't a bird but was an angel. The Dioscuri aspired to marry the Leucippides ("daughters of the white horse") and had children. Again, Jesus never married nor had children. Zeus requested that Pollux return to Olympus with him or choose to give half of his immortality to his brother. Pollux chose the latter and gave half his immortality to his brother Castor. The two were allowed to walk between Olympus and Hades until they died. Jesus had no brother to give "half" of his immortality to; however atheists claim that this symbolically shows the Christian idea of "eternal salvation". Sounds similar, however Pollux only gives half of his life to his brother and not to thousands of other people. Atheists point out that this character was able to descend to Hell like Jesus did. Again sounds similar but the truth is the idea that Jesus descended into Hell came from the Apostles Creed that apostles never had a hand in writing that reads: *"I believe that Jesus ... descended into hell."* Early Church scholars believed that Acts 2:31 described this. Read the following verse: *"Seeing what was to come, he spoke of the resurrection of the Messiah, that he was not abandoned to the realm of the dead, nor did his body see decay."* This verse clearly states that Jesus "was not abandoned to the realm of the dead." The realm of the dead that this verse is talking about is the grave and not Hell. Notice the rest of the verse states: "nor did his body see decay."

Some quote, 1 Peter 3:18-20 claiming that Jesus did go to Hell, however the traditional belief of evangelical Christians is that Jesus spoke “in spirit” through Noah as he built the Ark. It is the belief that the verse describes Jesus [as God] speaking a message of repentance and righteousness, during the time before the flood given to unbelieving people who were then on earth but now are "spirits in prison" [Hell].

Dionysus, His mother was a mortal woman, Semele, the daughter of king Cadmus of Thebes, and his father was Zeus, the king of the gods. Dionysus had no virgin birth and that being said the Virgin Mary wasn’t of a royal line like Semele was. In the story Hera (Zeus’ wife) appears as a bird to Semele. The Heavenly Father has no wife and again the Holy Spirit did not appear as a bird during Jesus’ birth. Atheists like to mock the baptism by saying that it is also recorded in this story by stating that Dionysus had two mothers, Semele and Zeus. When Hera killed Semele, Zeus took the baby Dionysus and sewed him into his thigh. In this version of the story Zeus releases Dionysus from his thigh on Mt. Pramnos. The thing is this isn’t a second birth, there was no water to be immersed in and it is silly to think that being born from a thigh has any relation to Christian baptism.

Thor, is the Germanic and Norse god of thunder. Thor married Sif and his father is Odin.

Although similar from only appearance, Thor was married and had many children as well as adulterous affairs with servants begetting other gods. Odin also had other sons who were siblings to Thor. Jesus was the only begotten Son of God, wasn't married, never had any adulterous affairs and never had any children. Thor's father Odin was originally the god the Celtic tribes until the Germans got a hold of him and applied Odin to their mythology.

The fact remains that there are a lot of difference between Jesus and heroes and saviors of mythology. The following is a table of major differences between mythological characters and the historical Jesus.

1. Mythological characters married and had children. Jesus did not.

2. Mythological characters were only half-gods and never claimed to be Zeus, while Jesus is the Son of God and part of the Godhead.

3. Mythological characters usually only died for one to three people, while Jesus died for everyone who would accept him.

4. Mythological characters died in various ways unknown to their own fate, Jesus died specifically to Old Testament prophecy and knew how he was going to die.

5. Mythological characters were begotten by fatherly gods through adultery in the disguise of birds. Jesus wasn't begotten by adultery and the Holy Spirit isn't described as a bird symbol until Jesus' baptism; no relation of a bird symbol is at Jesus' birth.

6. Mythological characters were killed in various ways other than the specific way Jesus died in the Gospels which all describe Jesus' death harmoniously.

7. Mythological characters had all kinds of enemies in their stories. Jesus has a specific enemy in the form of Satan.

8. Zeus had various half-god children. Jesus was the only begotten Son.

9. Mythological characters are faced with a jealous goddess who adds to their death. Jesus never had a jealous female who was the cause of his death.

10. Mythological characters had additional help in personal battles. Jesus generally defended himself mostly verbally. Those who tried to defend Jesus he criticized.

11. Mythological characters only performed single specific miraculous tasks. Jesus performed multiple miraculous tasks.

12. Mythological stories of heroic saviors only look similar to the story of Jesus from **only** an appearance.

There are over 500 worldwide accounts of a global flood and prior to the flood there was a prophecy made in the Garden of Eden that a messiah (a savior) would be sent to save mankind (Genesis 3:15). Also nearly every culture around the world has 12 signs in their zodiacs. In the Jewish zodiac called the "Mazzaroth" (Genesis 1:14; Job 36) depicts the seed of the virgin taking on the seed of the dragon. A fresco of sorts that God placed in the sky during creation with stars to show what will happen with humanity. The two seeds fight until the end when the "lion" [seed of the virgin] is in triumph. With every culture around the world describing a global flood, having similar stories of saviors and zodiacs strikingly similar, wouldn't you think that ancient man passed down an important prophecy after the flood? With each telling of the prophecy and each culture moving away from God aside from Abraham's line through Isaac, that it is possible that the prophecy was twisted like a phrase through the grape vine?

The fact is that the early church fathers who wrote content during early church times convicted pagan beliefs of worshipping false gods and didn't accept pagan gods into Christianity. The early church preached to pagan religions that what they were actually worshipping were demons. Take a look at what the 1st century (100-165) Christian evangelist Justin Martyr said about the worship of "gods".

"Not knowing that these spirits were demons, they called them 'gods,' and gave to each the name which each of the demons chose for himself."

Tatian, a 2nd century disciple of Justin Martyr and apologist said to the Greeks about god idols:

"The demons, as you call them, received their structure from matter and obtained the spirit which is inherent in it. As a result, they became intemperate and greedy...O Greeks, you worship these beings, produced from matter, but very remote from right conduct."

Mark Minucius Felix a 2nd century lawyer who convert to Christianity and became an apologist once said:

"As is shown by the Magi, the philosophers, and Plato, these impure spirits (the demons) lurk under the statues and images that are consecrated to them. In the meantime, they are

breathed into the [pagan] prophets. They dwell in the shrines, and they sometimes animate the fibers of the entrails. They control the flights of birds, direct the lots, and are the cause of oracles involved in many falsehoods."

The early church was completely against accepting any pagan doctrine into the fold of the church. They treated the "gods" of other pagan cults and religions as evil spirits and demons and preached against the worship of them. In a sense early Christian scholars knew that the doctrines of pagan worship were twisted doctrines and didn't accept them.

Christians Keep Changing the Bible

No, Christians do not keep changing or altering God's word. This is perceived due to the fact that there are so many versions of the Holy Bible. The reason why scholars and theologians continue to update the Bible is for the present time so that people who want to read it can understand it in either their own language or to meet the needs of the present slang. If you read the 1611 version of the King James Version (KJV) of the Bible would you completely understand it? Probably not, however the people in the early-sixteen hundreds could understand it. Christians that only like to stay with the King James Version wanted that version to be updated for themselves so a new version was "updated" called The New King James (NKJ) which still keeps the same overtones and is understandable in today's English. The New International Version or NIV is more up to date for our time to understand God's word.

Each new Bible still keeps the same important message that was spoken two thousand years ago and beyond so that people can generally grasp the message. Nothing has changed.

The Trinity is 3 gods and not 1 God

When people worship multiple gods this is called polytheism. The worship of a single god is called theism, and that is what Christianity is. Muslims, atheists and other religious traditions feel that Christians are polytheist due to the trinity of God. They see the trinity of God the Father, God the Son and God the Holy Spirit as three gods and not one. It isn't confusing when you understand water. Water is composed of two hydrogen atoms and one oxygen atom. Together they form a perfect "trinity" of H2O. Water also comes in three structures as either a liquid, a gas [vapor] or a solid [ice]. Either way you see it in whatever structure water is in it is still water. A perfect "trinity", the same but liquid water is not ice nor is it vapor. Ice is not liquid water, and not vapor, and vapor is not ice nor is it liquid water but still they are all water.

The earth is one planet but yet it contains an atmosphere, solid matter and water; three elements come together to form one celestial body. Some people see the trinity of God as 1+1+1=3; however after the logic I just gave you the trinity is more like this: 1x1x1=1.

Science Disproves the Bible

The word "science" means "knowledge", let's not forget that here when we bring up the Bible.

Science actually confirms the Bible very plainly. The Bible itself holds scientific knowledge that was penned thousands of years before scientist's unlocked discoveries. The Bible also held onto historical events that archeology has only recently discovered. You could say that if Scientists would have looked at the Bible before conducting research they could have went out and found it rather than making discoveries.

Archeological finds that are in the Bible

"In extraordinary ways, modern archeology is affirming the historical core of the Old and New Testaments, supporting key portions of crucial biblical stories."

– Jeffery L. Sheler.

"Scores of archeological findings have been made which confirm in clear outline of exact detail historical statements in the Bible."

– Dr. Nelson Glueck

"We do not know of any cases where the Bible has been proved wrong."

– Dr. Joesph P. Free

Those statements are so very true. The more archeology digs the more they reaffirm the scriptures of the Bible. The following is only a brief amount of the large discoveries archeology has made that confirm the Bible.

Only recently in our modern history has science discovered that the continents drifted apart. The Bible tells us **when** the continents broke apart (Genesis 10:25).

Hattusha, the capital city of the Hittite empire

The Bible makes more than 40 references to the Hittite Empire. For a long time skeptics thought that the Bible was in error since there was no archeological evidence for the Hittites. It wasn't until in 1906 when Hugo Winckler uncovered a huge library of 10,000 clay tablets which documented the Hittite Empire. The ancient Hittite capital was discovered about 90 miles east of Ankara, Turkey. The Hittites rule extended to Syria and Lebanon. The empire rivaled the Egyptian Empire. The Bible additionally told who founded the Hittite civilization (Genesis 10:15; 23:2-20; 25:8) a man named "Heth" and mentions the people. (Genesis 15:18;26:34; 27:46; 36:2; 49:29; 50:13; Numbers 13:29; Joshua 11:2 Judges 1:18; 3:5; Nehemiah 9:8...)

In times past skeptics use to say that King David never existed until 1993 when archeologists discovered a stone in Israel with inscriptions, "House of David" and "King of Israel" dated to the 9th century BC a century after David's reign and described a victory by a neighboring king over the Israelites. Now it is difficult for skeptics to say that David never existed.

The stone that tells about the House of David discovered in Israel in 1993/94. Now on display in the Israel Museum.

In 1990 archeologists discovered a first century tomb two miles from the Temple Mount. They discovered bones in the tomb of a man in his 60's with inscriptions "Yehosef bar Qayafa" meaning "Joseph, son of Caiaphas." Experts believe this was Caiaphas, the high priest who was involved in the arrest of Jesus and had him handed over to Pontius Pilate (Matthew 26:57-67).

In 1947 hundreds of scrolls and scraps were discovered dated 300 BC **to** AD 70 in the caves of Qumran near the Dead Sea seven miles south of Jericho. Most of the scrolls were over 1000 years old. They were older than most of the manuscripts scholars previously had available. The discovery of these scrolls was an important historical find because it revealed that the Bible had been copied over the years very accurately.

Scientific Facts found in the Bible

Only recently science has discovered that everything is composed of invisible atoms. The Bible in Hebrews 11:3 described thousands of years ago that the things seen were not made of things which do appear.

Medical science only recently discovered that blood-clotting in a newborn reaches its peak on the eighth day. The Bible consistently says that a new born male should be circumcised on the eighth day.

Around 1500 B.C. the scientists of the day believed that the earth sat on a giant animal, while the Bible spoke of the earth free floating in space (Job 26:7).

The Prophet Isaiah told us thousands of years ago that the earth is round (Isaiah 40:22). Do you recall a time in 1492 when people believed the earth was flat? It was only 2,400 years later from Isaiah that man discovered that the world wasn't flat.

In the mid 1970's most cosmologists, scientists who study the universe and its evolution agree that the initial void of the Genesis account of creation may be uncanny to the truth.

Centuries ago science would have people bled to remove disease. This was called bled letting which caused a lot of deaths. The Bible taught the importance of blood as the source of life 3,000 years ago (Leviticus 17:11).

These are just a few of the many scientific facts found in the Bible. But you get the idea, right? The knowledge for discoveries of today was given thousands of years ago by God in His word; divine inspiration of course. God gave many specific instructions that science is only discovering today out of love for us to help us through this tough journey called life. The knowledge and discoveries of today have been right in front of us for thousands of years.

Evolution is Proven

Actually no it is not. Scientists have yet to prove the theory of evolution. There are still to this day scientists who don't believe in it. British journalist and philosopher, Malcolm Muggeridge once said, *"I myself am convinced that the theory of evolution, especially the extent to which it has been applied, will be one of the great jokes in the history books of the future."*

Most of the popular scientists that atheists like to portray as atheists were actually curious about God's creation. Which is why they entered into scientific studies. Albert Einstein, a professing Jew said, *"I have repeatedly said that in my opinion the idea of a personal God is a childlike one, but I do not share the crusading spirit of the professional atheist whose fervor is mostly due to a painful act of liberation from the fetters of religious indoctrination received in youth. I prefer an attitude of humility corresponding to the weakness of our intellectual understanding of nature and of our own being."*

There is a continuing movement hard at work together to overturn the theory of evolution and present Intelligent Design in schools. Actually the truth is evolution is only a British and American idea that isn't shared with much of the world. There are parts of Canada and Africa that still teach Creation Science as well as most of the Middle East. Evolution is widely unpopular and 85% of Americans don't believe that humanity came from apes but instead just go with the flow of high school teachings on evolution in the classroom and do not accept it. The theory of evolution is actually a pressed upon doctrine on American society that no one wants nor believes in but a select few. Doesn't this logic reflect the notion of what the radical atheist movement says about Christianity?

Sir Arthur Keith, author of the Foreward to The Origin of the Species, 100th edition said, *"Evolution is **unproved and unprovable**. We* *believe it only because the only alternative is special creation, and that is unthinkable."*

This is an unwise statement to make. Why is special creation unthinkable? And why teach something that is "unprovable?" Look at what the Harvard paleontologist Steven Jay Gould once said, *"The extreme rarity of transitional forms in the fossil record persists as the* ***trade secret*** *of paleontology..."*

During an address at the American Museum of Natural History in New York City in 1981, Dr. Colin Patterson, a senior paleontologist at the British Museum of Natural History said this about the theory of evolution,

"One morning I woke up and ...it struck me that I had been working on this stuff for twenty years and there was not one thing I knew about it. That's quite a shock to learn that one can be misled so long...I've tried putting a simple question to various people: ***'Can you tell me anything you know about evolution, any one thing, any one thing that is true?*** *I tried that question on the geology staff at the Field Museum of Natural History and the* ***only answer I got was silence.*** *I tried it on the members of the Evolutionary Morphology Seminar in the University of Chicago, a very prestigious body of evolutionists,* ***and all I got there was silence for a long time*** *and eventually one person said, 'I do*

*know one thing - **it ought not to be taught in high school.**"*

The fact is that Creation and Evolution cannot co-exist. One of them is right while the other is wrong. One of them has overwhelming evidence while the other has not a shred of truth to it.

Dinosaurs Prove Evolution

Actually dinosaurs prove special creation. The word "dinosaur" means "terrible lizard" and is generally a "modern day term" applied to the discovery of dinosaurs. The word was first coined in 1841 as "Dinosauria" by the British anatomist Sir Richard Owen. The term quickly took root when referencing these creatures. When the first examinations of dinosaurs began in the 1800's, scientists failed to look at history to find out what happen to these creatures.

Dinosaurs have a much more ancient name that was given to them by our ancestors. The word "dragon" was actually the first title given to what we now call "dinosaurs". The Bible itself has over 42 references to the word "dragon". Early century dictionaries actually had "now rare" next to the definition of "dragon." Dragon history is universal throughout all the cultures of the world. What one other type of large lizard group definition is also universal? The knowledge of and definition of "dinosaur." The fact is that there were eye witnesses of dragons in history.

The images of the dragon what you know with legs and wings wasn't the style of dragon that was known during ancient times. The dragon you know with legs and wings is a creature made up from modern mythology.

There is even an old science book titled, "Historia Animalium" published at Zurich in 1551-58 and 1587 describes how "dragons" were **rare but not extinct** and were actually **small at that time**.

Image from Historia Animalium shows two legged dragons similar to dinosaurs we know of today as pterosaurs

The study of dragons is called "dracontology" and looks at the crypto-zoology and legends in the past. However, draconolotgy also looks at factual stories of eye witness accounts from historical legends.

Ever heard of the Terror of the Tarasque? This legend comes from France and says that the Tarasque was the spawn of the Biblical monster Leviathan and originally lived in Galatia, Asia Minor. The creature appeared near the banks of the River Rhone between Avignon and Arles in southern France. Images of this creature that residence states were passed down from their ancestors appear remarkably similar to a euoplocephalus or a glyptodon which were the size of a rhinoceros. A stone altarpiece, dating from 1470 in the Cathedral of Saint-Sauveur in Aix-en-Provence shows the dragon. 1470 is a far cry from 1790 when Gideon A. Mantell discovered the first dinosaur bones, identifying it and later naming it Iguanodon.

Illustration of Tarasque

Illustration of a Euoplocephalus that looks uncanny to Tarasque.

Speaking of Leviathan, the Bible depicts this dragon six times in the Book of Job 41:1-41:34; as well as Psalm 74; 104; and in Isaiah 27:1. The Leviathan is a powerful serpent type creature that is described very similar to a plesiosaur. There is also the Behemoth that the

Bible depicts in Job 40:15-24. Scientists like to say that the Bible is describing an elephant, but does an elephant have a tail as thick as a cedar tree? The only known creature to man with a tail as thick as a cedar tree is a diplodocid or a sauropod which according to evolution lived during the cretaceous period. The Book of Job was written from 1900 to 1700 BC during the time of the patriarchs which was the same time period as Abraham.

When we take a look at dinosaurs even more we can find that they actually disprove the theory of evolution. For example, just an hour's drive south of Fort Worth, Texas near a river named Paluxy that moved through the rocky wooded countryside near Glen Rose are human and dinosaur fossil tracks side by side. And get this, the cream-colored fossil-filled layers that the tracks are in is supposed to be of the "Cretaceous" period; the period evolutionists believe dinosaurs lived. Why are human fossilized tracks in the Cretaceous period? These fossil human prints are not worn down weathered dinosaur tracks like evolutionists would have you believe. You can actually see human toes, and you can take your shoes off and place your own foot in them perfectly.

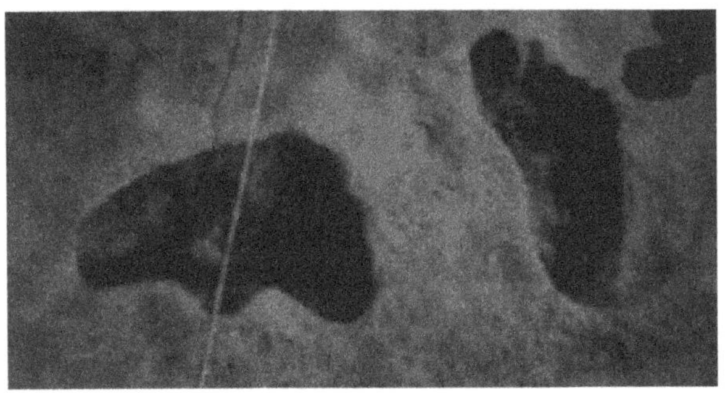

This photo was taken by the late Dr. Cecil Daugherty, in the 1970's near Paluxy River in Glen Rose, Texas. Photo clearly shows human and dinosaur footprints next to each other.

Consider for a moment there are pre-Colombian artifacts that reveal dinosaurs. There is a narrow strip of land between North and South America called the Isthmus of Panama, known in the past as the Isthmus of Darien. This is now called Panama and contains the Panama Canal. In this region were found artifacts. Evolutionists believe that that land bridge was formed three million years ago; however artifacts were discovered depicting what appears to be dinosaurs from the Cretaceous period. When these artifacts were found that look remarkably similar to dinosaurs, it caused many to question the entire evolutionary theory and materialistic time frame for the extinction of the dinosaurs.

You will be shocked to know that there is an overwhelming amount of physical evidence that reveals that dinosaurs and humans lived side by side.

In 1535 Spanish conquistadors journeyed through the area of the Nazca Indians [now Peru] and discovered stones with strange images on them of what appeared to be dinosaurs. Of the 16,000 stones only 500 had carvings of images that look exactly like what we know today as dinosaurs.

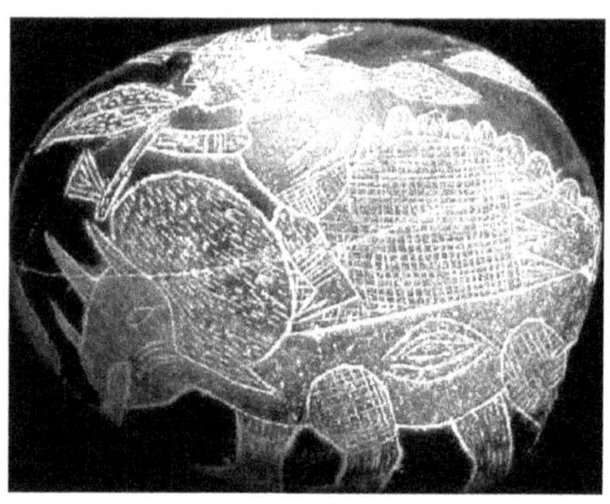

Nazca stone reveals a clear portrait of a man riding on the back of a triceratops. These stones were merely just the Nazca's observations of everyday life in their culture.

If you still don't believe that man and dinosaurs lived at the same time or were still relatively around, then read the account of Marlo Polo.

"Leaving the city of Yachi, and traveling ten days in a westerly direction, you reach the province of Karazan, which is also the name of the chief city....Here are seen huge serpents, ten paces in length (about 30 feet), and ten spans (about 8 feet) girt of the body. At the fore part, near the head, they have two short legs, having three claws like those of a tiger, with eyes larger than a forepenny loaf (pane da quattro denari) and very glaring."

The jaws are wide enough to swallow a man, the teeth are large and sharp, and their whole appearance is so formidable, that neither man, nor any kind of animal can approach them without terror. Others are met with of a smaller size, being eight, six, or 5 paces long; and the following method is used for taking them. In the day-time, by reason of great heat, they lurk in caverns, from whence, at night, they issue to seek their food, and whatever beast they meet with and can lay hold of, whether tiger, wolf, or any other, they devour;

"After which they drag themselves towards some lake, spring of water, or river, in order to drink. By their motion in this way along the shore, and their vast weight, they make a deep impression, as if a heavy beam had been drawn along the

sands. Those whose employment is to hunt them observe the track by which they are most frequently accustomed to go, and fix into the ground several pieces of wood, armed with sharp iron spikes, which they cover with sand in such a manner as not to be perceptible.

When therefore the animals make their way towards the places they usually haunt, they are wounded by these instruments, and speedily killed. The crows, as soon as they perceive them to be dead, set up to scream; and this serves as a signal to the hunters, who advance the spot, and proceed to separate the skin from the flesh, taking care immediately to secure the gall, which is most highly esteemed in medicine.

In cases of the bite of a mad dog, a penny weight of it, dissolved in wine, is administered. It is also useful in accelerating parturition, when the labor pains of women have come on. A small quantity of it being applied to carbuncles, pustules, or other eruptions on the body, they are presently dispersed; and it is efficacious in many other complaints.

The flesh also of the animal is sold at a dear rate, being thought to have a higher flavor than other kinds of meat, and by all persons it is esteemed a delicacy."

Doesn't this type of animal sound like a carnasaur? A Carnasaur is group of dinosaurs that tyrannosaurs and allosaurs belong to. It would appear that the historical evidence is there that dragons and dinosaurs are one in the same.

So what really happen to the dinosaurs? Throughout many cultures around the world there are over 500 stories of a global flood. Although most of the dinosaurs were wiped out, Noah had to have taken either eggs or young dinosaurs onto the ark. This makes sense since younger dinosaurs would eat less food, create less waste, sleep more and be more fertile for reproductive purposes.

After the flood the population of the dinosaurs flourished once again. However, the harsh weather conditions resulting from the flood mixed with the terrible carnivorous and destructive attributes of these creatures plagued humanity and caused massive hunts killing off much of these creatures. We can see in the Marco Polo account and other legends of warriors fighting dragons, such as the story of St. George that dragons were destructive and were hunted for sport, status and cures for disease. Over time the dinosaurs became rare and were only spoke about in stories until no one was able to find them anymore and they fell into legend. That is until the first discovery of dinosaur bones and scientists decided to come up with their own ideas on where these creatures came from ignoring the historical record completely.

Religion is Violent and Causes War

What if I told you that man is violent and causes war? If a human being believes in a doctrine with extreme measure no matter if that doctrine is good or evil, humanity will in some way find a wicked way to abuse that doctrine and force it upon others. Christianity itself on the other hand doesn't force its doctrines on people, it is a choice when it is presented to an individual to choose to love God or not. A loving God would not force a person to love him, which is the essence of why we have freewill.

For centuries man has used religion as a tool for war. The Nazi's had "God with us" on their belt buckles and American soldiers sang, "Praise the Lord and pass the Ammunition" during World War 2. The fact is everyone around the world wants God on **their** side on an issue but never consider the scriptures to know what God actually thinks over an issue.

The men and women who have wickedness in their heart [which is everyone] will become radical upon how they "present" a religion onto a people. They will look inside their cruel hearts to entice and deceive people to believe in a doctrine and control them; which is the cause of most atheists. People who have been harmed in some way by a radical religious idea will usually become turned off by religion and become either agnostic or atheist.

Radicals can be in every religion as well as atheism also. There are radical movements by atheists to force prayer out of schools, remove God from government, and stop people from practicing services at public gatherings. If we take a look at agnostic and atheism societies from history such as China, The Soviet Union and Nazi Germany we can find that the structure of these societies collapsed with the removal of God.

Christians are Narrow Minded

Yes we are. Christians intentionally become narrow minded by sticking to the scriptures to protect themselves from false teaching and erroneous thinking. Christians in a sense want the truth and look for it much like you are now. Most Christians were like you, seeking the truth by investigating philosophies and science for themselves. Humans have been seeking truth since ancient times and Pontius Pilate even stated this human question in response to Jesus' statement. Pilate said "What is truth?" (John 18:38) This question has haunted humanity for ages.

Christian narrow mindedness has helped whole civilizations to understand what is evil and immoral to prevent the downfall of societies but still other religious immoral groups want openness in society to practice their form of religion. A great example of openness is the nation of Haiti which is plagued with poverty due to the fact that they invited false teachings and use resources unwisely.

The fact is Christianity is the foundation of western civilization, and as a result the western world has become more advanced than any civilization in history due to Christian principles. If it wasn't for Christianity your life would be greatly different. You wouldn't be free and could live in some negative barbaric society with cult-like religious doctrines forced upon you like Islam. Christianity has and always will be a choice for people. The fact remains that when there are religious uprisings most non-believers claim to be Christian in the west even though they never went to church. This is because everyone recognizes that Christianity had a large hand in the formation of western society.

There is a 40 Year Gap

What this statement refers to is that after Jesus ascended into heaven, everyone forgot, and then 40 years later everyone remembered again due to Paul's ministry. The fact is there isn't a 40 year gap. Even if there was, 40 years would still be enough to say that something historical happened. If a 40 year gap itself was not enough to present historical fact then the periods that paleontologist describe in prehistoric times cannot be accurate since there are a thousand to millions of years of guessing. How then can a thousand or million year gaps prove the theory of evolution? There is more evidence to support that Jesus existed than there is to prove the prehistoric time frames suggested by evolutionists that place the dinosaurs.

The Arch of Titus in Rome, which shows the treasures taken from the Temple in Jerusalem.

One thing to consider is the fact that in AD 66-70 the Roman army under Emperor Titus invaded Jerusalem and leveled the temple. The Jews fled to other parts of the empire such as Alexandria, Carthage and Rome which caused Antioch to be the center for Christianity. According to the Book of Acts the Church began in Jerusalem (Acts 2:5-50) and stayed there for a long period of time until the Romans invaded. Entire cities were wiped out and we can see the level of destruction by looking at the temple mount today. We know this happened by looking at the Arch of Titus in Rome, which shows the treasures taken from the Temple in Jerusalem, including the menorah and the trumpets of Jericho. The Romans utterly destroyed and leveled an entire large temple. Of course it is possible that any evidence of Jesus could have been destroyed during this invasion and fleeing of the Jews. Eye witnesses who personally knew Jesus could have been killed which would have greatly reduced the amount of eye witness testimony. Those who would have survived may have been terrified by such an invasion, went into hiding or mixed in with the church in other provinces.

The overwhelming evidence for the existence of Jesus Christ both in secular and Biblical history is the fact that in the 1st century AD there were thousands including the apostles who were willing to be martyred for Jesus Christ. The fact is people would die for what they believe in. Why would any of these early Christians die for a lie?

The truth about the New Testament writings is that it is a well-known fact that much of the New Testament was **composed** (being written) before AD 62 (30 years after Jesus' death). Atheists claim that Paul didn't start writing his letters until 70 AD. How is that possible when Paul was dead at this time? Paul died at the hands of Emperor Nero and Nero's reign lasted from 13 October 54 to 9 June 68. Much of the New Testament letters was in the process of their compositions 30 years after Jesus died. We know from Josephus that James (James the Just), the first bishop of Jerusalem, Jesus' brother was killed in AD 62 (Acts 12:2). So we can conclude, beyond reasonable doubt that the book of Acts was written before AD 62. If Acts was written in AD 62 then that would mean that the Gospel of Luke was composed before that. In Luke's second book called Acts he states to a person named Theophilus, "in my former book, Theophilus, I wrote about all that Jesus began to do and to teach..." (Acts 1:1-4) By this very statement in the book of Acts we know for a fact that the Gospel of Luke was being composed between AD 37 and AD 41. Should this be true and accurate then there is actually a 4 - 8 year gap making the Gospel of Luke the most accurate historical account of Jesus' existence.

There is No Historical Evidence for Jesus

Actually there is. Not to mention what we just discussed about a 4 - 8 year gap instead of a 40 year gap there are over 39 ancient sources in addition to the New Testament. For one the evidences are in the form of the gospels themselves composed at very accurate dates. Now before you say, "But they are in the Bible and I don't believe the Bible." The Bible has been recognized by archeologists for its historical value. Do you recall the previous archeological facts we provided? The gospels are historically accurate just as the Apocrypha books of the Maccabees that tell the story of the plight of the Jews against the Greeks.

Tacitus Letter

One of the most important sources outside of the historically accurate New Testament is from Emperor Nero's decision to blame the Christians for the fire that had destroyed Rome in A.D. 64, the Roman historian Tacitus wrote:

"Nero fastened the guilt . . . on a class hated for their abominations, called Christians by the populace. Christus, from whom the name had its origin, suffered the extreme penalty during the reign of Tiberius at the hands of . . . Pontius Pilatus, and a most mischievous superstition, thus checked for the moment, again broke out not only in Judaea, the first source of the evil, but even in Rome. . . ."

Notice that Tacitus says, "suffered the extreme penalty" obviously alluding to the Roman method of execution known as crucifixion. That fact that Tacitus mentions that this happen during the reign of Tiberius upholds the historical accuracy of the Gospel accounts. Tacitus' describes the conviction of the early church by the Roman authority which is a very important point for evidence of the early church. This testimony also depicts a rapidly growing religion which coincides with Acts 16:5, "So the churches were strengthened in the faith and grew daily in numbers."

Pliny Letter

One other piece of evidence to support the early Church dated A.D. 112 is from Pliny the Younger who wrote to Emperor Trajan about how to prosecute people for being Christians.

"They were in the habit of meeting on a certain fixed day before it was light, when they sang in alternate verses a hymn to Christ, as to a god, and bound themselves by a solemn oath, not to any wicked deeds, but never to commit any fraud, theft or adultery, never to falsify their word, nor deny a trust when they should be called upon to deliver it up; after which it was their custom to separate, and then reassemble to partake of food--but food of an ordinary and innocent kind."

There are several important points in this historical piece that reveals how the early Church operated. One, they met on a fixed day of the week, two, they sang hymns to Christ revealing the early Church's belief in Jesus and affirming their belief in His divinity. Notice that the reference says, "…hymn to Christ, as to a god…" this is a clear point that unlike gods of the day who were worshipped, Jesus was worshipped as god who lived. Should this reference be correct, Pliny understood that what the Christians were worshipping during those days was God. This agrees perfectly with the testimonies with the New Testament. Pliny's account of the early Christians provides us a reference of the practices of the early church that they held a high moral standard and kept the 10

Commandments which is a very Jewish tradition to do. Also notice that Pliny references the "love feast" stating, "but food of an ordinary and innocent kind." The early church was battling with non-Christians over accusations of "ritual cannibalism" practices. The early Christians humbly obverted these slanderous accusations against Jesus' own teaching.

Antiquitates Iudaice libri XX, De bello Iudaico libri VII by Titus Flavius Josephus

les g... donné,&sans aucune difference donnoient de grands coups de bastons tant à
ceux qui ne disoient mot, qu'à ceux qui faisoient le bruit. Ces pauures gens qui
estoient sans armes ne bastons, furent ainsi traitez inhumainement : aucuns furent occis les autres s'en retournerent blessez : & par ce moyen le bruit fut ap-
paisé.
En ce mesme temps estoit Iesus, homme sage, si toutefois il est licite de l'ap-
peller homme. Car il faisoit des œuures admirables: & estoit precepteur de ceux
qui oyent & recoiuent volôtiers choses vrayes: lequel eut beaucoup de disciples
qui le suiuoient tât des Iuifs que des Gentils. C'estoit le Christ: & les principaux
gouuerneurs de nostre nation l'accuserent deuât Pilate, lequel le côdâna a estre
crucifié. Quelque chose qu'il y eust, ceux qui auoient côméncé à l'aimer, ne lais-
serét de l'aymer pour l'ignominie de sa mort: car il leur apparut vif le troisiesme
iour apres: ce que les Prophetes diuinement inspirez auoient predit de luy, auec
plusieurs autres choses grandes & merueilleuses: & iusques à ce iourd'huy il y a
vne racé de Chrestiens qui durent encore, lesquels ont prins ce nom de luy.
Enuiron ce temps là les Iuifs furent troublez d'vne autre fascherie : & à Rome aduint vn cas vilain & deshonneste qui n'estoit gueres dissemblable, ainsi
qu'on faisoit le seruice diuin d'Isis. Ie parleray donc de ce forfait execrable,
en premier lieu, & puis ie poursuiuray les faits des Iuifs. Il y auoit à Rome vne
femme laquelle on nommoit Pauline, femme bien renommée tant pour sa
vie honneste, que pour la noblesse de son parentage: & outre tout cela, elle
estoit riche & belle, comme estant en la fleur de son aage : mais sur toutes ses
vertus elle estoit ornee de pudicité mariée à Saturnin homme digne d'vne telle
femme. Vn certain ieune homme nommé Decius Mundus, lequel auoit assez
bon renom entre les cheualiers, fut esprins de l'amour de ceste femme: & pour-
ce que le cœur d'icelle estoit tel qu'il ne pouuoit estre facilement corrompu par
dons, tât plus estoit la rage de cest amoureux embrasée tellemét qu'il luy offroit
iii
Tome 1.

A page from the Testimonium Flavianum by Titus Flavius Josephus

Jewish Historian Josephus

One of the most remarkable references to the historical Jesus is the writings from the Jewish historian Titus Flavius Josephus (37 – 100), also called Joseph ben Matityahu. A lot of mainstream atheists try to tell people that this account has been proven to be a fraud. However, the fact is that the account by Josephus is only questioned by a "few" scholars to not have been penned by the historian. “Most” scholars and historians believe the account is a factual and historical account. But why did “few” scholars believe that the account wasn’t penned by Josephus? These few scholars even believe that Josephus “wrote” the historical account of Jesus. The problem is that it was altered in the second or third century A.D. by a Christian. However, scholars point out that Josephus wasn’t a Christian and the fact remains that the account was originally recorded by a non-believing, non-Christian!

Josephus recorded two accounts but the astonishing is called the "Testimonium Flavianum," the relevant portion declares:

“About this time there lived Jesus, a wise man, if indeed one ought to call him a man. For he . . . wrought surprising feats. . . . He was the Christ. When Pilate . . .condemned him to be crucified, those who had . . . come to love him did not give up their affection for him. On the third day he appeared . . . restored to life. . . . And the tribe of Christians . . . has . . . not disappeared.”

The problem that few scholars have with this account is that the statement “a wise man” seems appealing to Jesus but the phrase “if indeed one ought to call him a man” and the

"Christ" statements seems suspect and that Josephus being a Jew would even state Jesus to be the Christ which means "messiah". It is this phrase that few scholars believe that was altered by an early Christian. However, scholars point out that Josephus wasn't a Christian and as a historian still wrote about Jesus. Furthermore, scholars point out that the statements in the Testimonium Flavianum "on the third day he appeared" and "restored to life" couldn't have come from a non-Christian which Josephus was!

Even though we remove the Josephus historical account we are still left with circumstantial evidence for the resurrection of Jesus Christ. In a court of law a person can be convicted of a crime based on circumstantial evidence just as Timothy McVeigh was for the Oklahoma City bombing on June 11, 2001. The circumstantial evidence for the resurrection of Jesus Christ:

1. The evidence of the skeptics who were most hostile to Jesus prior to his death and became his supporters afterwards.

2. The importance of the Jewish religious rituals of offering an animal sacrifice and obeying the Mosaic Law. Within 5 weeks of Jesus' death there were more than 10,000 Jews suddenly and mysteriously abandoned these rituals. This abandonment of their national identity reveals that something significant happen.

3. We see the evidence of new rituals of Communion and Baptism in which the early Jews baptized in the name of the Father, the Son and Holy Ghost raising Jesus to God status.

4. We see the evidence of the quick rise of the Church after Jesus' death, spreading to the door of Rome and beyond. In the end the entire Roman Empire was changed fulfilling Old Testament prophecy by the prophet Daniel (Dan. 2).

5. And the most convincing circumstantial evidence of all is the fact that the disciples were willing to die for their beliefs. During the final days of their life they continuously went without food, they were mocked when they witnessed in foreign locations, beaten and thrown in prison. Each of the disciples except for one were martyred.

The Talmud

In a collection of Jewish writings called the Talmud reveals additional evidence for the historical evidence for the Jewish Jesus. The following significant evidence is taken from AD 70-200.

"On the eve of the Passover Yeshu was hanged. For forty days before the execution took place, a

herald . . . cried, He is going forth to be stoned because he has practiced sorcery and enticed Israel to apostasy."

This is a significant Jewish account. Notice the name "Yeshu" [Yeshua] which is Hebrew for the Greek version "Jesus" that we use today. This reference also shows that Jesus was hung and executed, which is a synonym for the Gospels account that Jesus was "crucified" to be executed. This account of "hung" was a term used to reference "crucifying" as in Galatians 3:31 that declares that Jesus was "hanged" as well as Luke 23:39 that tells about criminals who were "hung" in reference to crucifixion. Also notice the phrase, "he has practiced sorcery" which is a clear reference to his performance of miracles. The Talmud also reveals, "enticed Israel to apostasy." The early denominations of the Pharisees and Sadducees had difference of opinion over the teachings of Moses. Traditions were held among the two groups that went excessively above what Moses taught. When Jesus interpreted the Law of Moses to these two groups and his followers these two groups became angry with Jesus and believed that he was teaching apostasy which is defined as "erroneous teaching!" This fits with the Gospel accounts of the priests and Levites becoming upset with Jesus for teaching what they believed was heresy! Heresy and blasphemy was also met with "stoning" which we see a reference of this in the Talmud as well, "He is going forth to be stoned." This may be a clear indication to the priests and Levites plot to have Jesus killed. If so, then the Roman intervention changed their plans.

The account of the Talmud also trumps the idea that atheists have that Paul was the actually founder of Christianity and not Jesus. This is a Jewish account from the Talmud and not a Christian one. We can conclude here that Paul was not the founder of Christianity. At the same time we know from the Gospels as from Josephus that there were other disciples who personally knew Jesus preaching and teaching. Josephus mentions in one of his Jewish Antiquities the condemnation of one "James" by the Jewish Sanhedrin. Josephus specifically mentions that this James is "the brother of Jesus the so-called Christ." This matches Paul's description of James in Galatians 1:19 as "the Lord's brother." James was also a disciple of Jesus.

Evidence from Lucian

Lucian of Samosata was a second century Greek satirist who wrote of the early Church.

The Christians . . . worship a man to this day-- the distinguished personage who introduced their novel rites, and was crucified on that account. . . . [It] was impressed on them by their original lawgiver that they are all brothers, from the moment that they are converted, and deny the gods of Greece, and worship the crucified sage, and live after his laws.

Although Lucian makes his reference to the early Church disciples he does point out that "they worship a man who introduced their novel rites", which is a clear reference to Jesus who gave his teachings to his disciples and passed them onto new converts. This also fits nicely with circumstantial evidence for the resurrection of Jesus that we talked about earlier. Although Lucian doesn't give this person's name he further explains "and was crucified on that account." is referring clearly to the account that Jesus was crucified for the heresy that he taught that the Jewish leaders took offense. This fits nicely with the Gospel accounts of Jesus' contemporaries having him crucified for his teachings. Lucian also mentions that each convert is considered a brother upon their conversion. No other religion at that time taught that type of brotherhood. This conversion involved denying the Greek gods and following and worshipping the person who was crucified. It isn't that hard to imagine who this person was and that type of teaching would get anyone killed. Although Lucian doesn't mention it we can imply that by Lucian mentioning they denied the Greek gods, worshipped Jesus and followed his teachings that the early Christians believed that Jesus was more than just a human.

Paul Didn't Know about Jesus' Ministry

Such a statement was started by a movie producer who is also an atheist. This statement is also filled with enough holes that it doesn't hold water. These atheists also believe that Paul either founded Christianity or was solely alone in teaching the early doctrines. The fact is there were more apostles who knew Jesus personally and teaching people than just Paul. Paul even talks about James the brother of Jesus (Galatians 1:19) as does the Jewish historian Josephus. Paul also knew of the life of Jesus from these same apostles. Paul didn't like to refer himself as an apostle as equal as the twelve of Jesus, although in his letters to the churches he does refer himself as an apostle. However, Paul references himself as an apostle in the full translation of the term meaning "missionary" or "those who have been sent out." Paul was "sent out" many times by the church to whole cities to start churches and convert people (Acts 13:2,3; 15). Paul himself was a humble man, a tentmaker (Acts 18:3) and very knowledgeable in the laws of the Jews (Acts 22:3; Galatians 1:12). He was taught by a Jewish leader named Gamaliel, a leading authority of the Sanhedrin (The same authority that arrested and tried Jesus) and like many of the early Jewish Christians held onto Jewish teachings before realizing that the new covenant was a new law that adopted the Mosaic Law and trumped it. On a side note Gamaliel was one of the Jewish leaders who pleaded with the Sanhedrin to refrain from slaying Jesus (Acts 5:34–39). Nevertheless there were arguments among the early churches namely the famous Antioch and Jerusalem churches over the circumcision of gentiles in the church (Acts 15). These Christians finally realized that the gospel wasn't for just the Jews but for everyone as well and that gentiles didn't need to be circumcised.

Paul was a hard headed Jew who had a temper at times but was slowly caving to the new doctrine from his Jewish beliefs. He still held onto them like the other apostles and became energized to invite new converts that were gentles into the fold of the church.

Paul himself was strongly against the new religious movement that was sparked by Jesus' death and resurrection. At first Paul hated Christians and would search for them and once found he would have them executed (Acts 8:1–3; 9:13; 26:10; Galatians 1:13–14; Philippians 3:6). Paul consented to the death of the evangelist Stephen who was the first martyr of Christianity (Acts 7:58; 8:1; 22:20). How could a Jew like Paul who was so zealous to persecute Christians start a new religion? This is due to the fact that Jesus had a personal involvement in Paul's conversion which can be dated to AD 31–36 (Acts 9:1–31; 22:1–22; 26:9–24).

Many people who believe that Jesus and Paul contradicted each other in their teachings point out verses between the two. However, when faced with the teachings of individuals in the Bible the **entire context** of a teaching has to be taken into account. A verse is like a jewel in a ring and the band of the ring is its setting which is like the context. The fact is that Paul never contradicted Jesus but in a sense Paul finished Jesus' sentences with reassurance and implication. If we want to say that Jesus and Paul contradicted each other then it can be easy to say that Peter contradicted his own two sermons in Acts; even though they sound different they are in perfect harmony to message of salvation.

Another aspect to think about while reading the context between Paul's and Jesus' teachings is to consider the groups that the two were dealing with. Jesus was speaking to Sadducee and Pharisee Jews while Paul was dealing mostly with gentiles from other countries. Of course each person's teachings are going to be slightly different toward certain people from various cultures and traditions, however the teachings are completely the same just said in a different variation. When Paul traveled to foreign lands he would even have people with him who knew Jesus.

The Bible is Filled with Fairy Tales

If so then why are their Jews? If the Bible is a big fairy tale then why does the peoples and nations that the Bible historically depicts exist and existed in the ancient past? If the Bible were filled with fairy tales then the Jewish people didn't leave Egypt, there wouldn't be gas in your car because there wouldn't be Arabs. Truth is known that Arabs are descendants of Ishmael a son of Abraham from the Bible.

When you say that the Bible is filled with fairy tales you are saying that Jews, who have carried the Old Testament throughout history, don't exist. What is the consistent theme that runs through the Bible? Don't know? The Old Testament is God's promise to destroy death, and the New Testament reveals how he did it.

The Bible is traditionally about one person through the beginnings of creation, to law, to prophecy and prophecy and revelation being revealed. That person is in the form of Jesus Christ.

I Blasphemed Against the Holy Spirit

Atheists generally state the following, *"I renounce the Holy Spirit."* to define their version of blasphemy against the Holy Spirit. This comes from Jesus' statement in Mark 3:29 after he casts out demons and is accused by Jewish scribes for casting out demons with Beelzebub instead of the Spirit of God. There statement was a doubt of Jesus' work. The actions of Jesus weren't to just perform miracles but to allow the Holy Spirit to work so that people could hear the message. If a person was once saved but later decided to become an atheist making the statement above doesn't get them out of being saved. They were once already convicted and filled with acceptance for Jesus giving God a legal right over them. If a person is saved and denies Christ, then lives a long life as an atheist but decided to come back to Jesus there salvation is still genuine.

What blasphemy of the Holy Spirit actually is "the denial of the works of the Holy Spirit." To become saved it takes the "conviction of sin" (John 16:8) by the Holy Spirit. This is pretty much toward those people who the gospel message has never reached.

1 Corinthians 2:2-14 says, "The person without the Spirit does not accept the things that come from the Spirit of God but considers them foolishness, and cannot understand them because they are discerned only through the Spirit."

Acts 7:51 reveals the type of people who blaspheme against the Holy Spirit. Those who are "stiffed necked and uncircumcised in the heart and …always resist the Holy Ghost." When a person resists the Holy Spirit that person isn't allowing themselves to be saved and the Holy Spirit can't convict them of sin. Without conviction of sin there is no salvation and without salvation there is damnation (Mark 16:16). For those people who haven't been saved and speak that phrase, "I deny the Holy Spirit" still has the opportunity to accept Jesus as their Lord and Savior when their heart stops resisting him. So you can see how silly it is to make statements renouncing the Holy Spirit when the sin itself is merely just resisting the works of the Spirit of God until a person's heart is made humble.

Logically Thinking Reasonably

Where is your Evidence?

One of the statements that atheists like to make about God is that there isn't any evidence for him. 70% of Americans are Christians because they have had in some way a personal experience with a supernatural experience that defies all logic and reason. If something is commonly experienced by 70% of Americans then for someone to say there is no God should have undeniable proof that there is no God who created the universe. A person would actually have to travel to every part of the universe, search and return with undeniable proof that there isn't a creator.

An overwhelming example of people who have had supernatural experiences is the growth of the paranormal community. Millions of people around of the world have claims of being touched in some way by a ghost or spirit. They want to know specifically what these spirits or ghosts are so they educate themselves on how to use devices that can detect electromagnetic fields. They will investigate claims, conduct research and continue to discover more evidence for an afterlife. This solidifies the doctrines of nearly all religious teachings around the world that there is an afterlife.

Did you know Christianity Protects Atheists from the Evils of the World?

You must also consider the fact that while you are an atheist Christianity is actually helping you to freely think and come against religion. If it wasn't for Christianity you would not be able to speak out and be free to do so. Christianity is the religion that holds back the radical Islamic movement through evangelism and its martyrs. The more the atheist movement tries hard to remove and attack Christianity the more the atheist agenda helps radical Islam. If Islam were to take over the west, Shariah Law would prevent you from speaking against the prophet of Islam.

Why Attack just Christianity?

Why is it that Christianity is only attacked by atheists? Although atheists claim to attack all religions, we never hear about attacks on Islam, Buddhism and other religions. These attacks by atheists only solidify Christianity's prophesies of persecution toward Christians. In doing so draws more people into the fold of the Church.

Take off your Cloths

If human beings came from apes and animals are naked even though mammals have fur but still are naked, then what is stopping you from walking in public in the nude? The Bible says in Genesis that man was once naked but ate of the forbidden fruit and saw his shame and nakedness. Adam and Eve fashioned covers out of fig leaves and God later gave them animal skins as clothing. This is still evident today by **you** wearing clothing. Now you might be thinking, "We wear clothing to stay warm." You're right but what is stopping people in warmer climates and around the world from wearing clothing? African and South American tribes who wear very little clothing still say that they would feel "exposed" or "shamed" if they removed what little coverings that they have. So

I ask you. Where did this shame come from? Why can't you expose yourself like animals do? That is because you are made in the image and likeness of God. You are an intelligent, thinking being that can solve problems and puzzles unlike animals. And unlike animals you have the knowledge of good and evil and are capable of performing such actions.

What is in a Name?

Why is it that all races around the world who didn't know each other during ancient times call themselves "Man?" This is because the human race had to have been "named" by a celestial source of divinity.

Why can't you Trust the Gospels?

There are only 7 manuscripts written over 1,000 years ago that survived of Plato's works and 643 of Homer's Iliad and yet no one has a problem trusting them. These works by Plato and Homer were written many times over throughout the centuries. Yet the Bible has over 24,000 manuscripts over time and atheists don't want to trust it? With the discovery of the Dead Sea Scrolls scholars discovered that the Holy Scriptures, compared today were in unchanged form. So what is the problem?

The Truth about Atheism

The fact remains that there are people who **just** don't want to believe. No matter the mountains of evidence for God and authenticity of the Bible by archeology and science, atheists still don't want to believe because of a simple childish fact. If there is a God then they would have to stop doing what they like and want to do. They see the Bible as a threat to their openness, free thinking and logic of reason, so they attack and counter the authenticity of the Holy Scriptures with much hatred to try and intimidate Christians and statesmen. Sound radical to you?

What about the Hebrew God?

Even if atheists were successful in proving beyond a shadow of a doubt that Jesus never existed (which is unlikely), there is still the Jewish belief in God to deal with. Jews don't share the same belief about Jesus as Christians do, however the God of the Old Testament is still there waiting for any attempt for atheists to disprove him. The Old Testament itself, as you have read from this book is loaded with archeological and scientific evidence that shows man was touched by some divine experience. In a nutshell my dear friend, God is still here.

Will Christianity ever go away?

Christianity is still the #1 religious movement around the world. Christianity has more followers than Islam, Buddhism and other religions. The Church continues to evangelize, and in so doing there are people who are martyred so that others will hear the gospel. The fact is humanity knows there is something wrong with willful sin, and in the process man wants redemption from doing wrong. He knows deep down that he cannot redeem himself, and when our hearts hear about Jesus and what he did for us we feel redeemed when we accept him. The majority of the world knows that Christianity is a positive source for mankind. Why remove a positive and moral source for humanity? If there wasn't any Christianity, if Jesus never died on the cross for our sins, we would still be in our sins and in danger for the wrath to come. The world would look much more negative and dangerous without the life, death, and resurrection of Jesus.

Isadora Duncan, an American Dancer said: "Art is not necessary at all. All that is necessary to make this world a better place to live in is to love--to love as Christ loved..."

Chuck Norris, a martial artists and movie star, said: "Real men do live for Christ. It is important to make your peace with Christ while the opportunity exists. Life is so fragile that you never know when it's going to be over. It could be over in the blink of an eye, and then it's too late to accept God's gift of salvation."

Albert Einstein said about why he studied science: "I want to know how God created things."

Frederick Chiluba, President (Zambia; from first free election) said: "Jesus was never against politics. He just wants us to recognize that there is a greater power above. We must all recognize there is a King of kings and a Lord of Lords, Jesus Christ, who is above every political system."

Vladimir Putin, President of Russia said: "Why did Christ come into the world? To liberate people from sickness, troubles, from death. In its essence, Christmas is a holiday of hope."

The thing is important figures from around the world know that there is hope for humanity in Jesus Christ. Without Jesus there is no hope.

How to get Saved

Do you consider yourself to be a good person? If you died right now where would you go? Heaven of Hell?

Have you ever lied? Have you ever stolen anything? Jesus said, if you have looked at someone in lust you have committed adultery. Have you committed adultery? If you have done any of these you are a liar, a thief and an adulterer and those are only 3 of the 10 Commandments and I haven't even gotten to the other 7. When you break the 10 Commandments you are offending a just and holy God. He loves you but there is no one higher than him and he has to judge sin. God doesn't send people to Hell, we send ourselves there when we sin. Based on the moral law of the 10 Commandments, if you died right now would you go to Heaven or Hell? Most likely Hell. You see if a judge is a good judge he couldn't let a murderer go in a court of law. If he was a good judge then he would have to throw the book at the murderer and place him in prison. God, as a good judge can't let you go free for breaking the moral law. This is why he sent Jesus to die on the cross for you and I. Jesus took your sins so that you might live (John 3:16,17).

To be saved all you have to do is pray a prayer of salvation and let the Holy Spirit guide you through your prayer. Then get baptized and change your life for the better. Put away your old life and do your best to live a better positive life.

Notes

http://www.bible.ca/trinity/trinity-pagan-christianity.htm

http://www.christianitytoday.com/ct/2000/february7/31.74.html

http://www.forbidden-history.com/dinosaur-movie.html

Time Magazine, December, 1976

Time Magazine, December, 1995

Readers Digest, June 2000

1999, Jeffrey L. Sheler, HarperCollins Publishers, Is the Bible True?

The Travels of Marco Polo, 1948 Book s; Chapter 40, pg. 185-186

Unlocking the Mysteries of Creation, Premium Edition, Dennis R. Petersen, 2002, Bride-Logos Publishers

Rose Book of Bible Charts, Maps & Time Lines

1998, A Dictionary of Early Christian Beliefs, David Bercot, Hendrickson Publishers, Inc.

2003, Dragons, A Natural History, Dr. Karl Shuker, Barnes & Noble, Inc.

www.ingramcontent.com/pod-product-compliance
Ingram Content Group UK Ltd.
Pitfield, Milton Keynes, MK11 3LW, UK
UKHW020218250726
13967UKWH00001B/64

9 781300 285311